TEACHER MAGIC

WRITTEN BY MICHELLE GANO
ILLUSTRATED BY STEFANIE GEYER

Teacher Magic

Copyright © 2021 Michelle Gano

All rights reserved. No part of this publication may be reproduced, distributed, or transmitted in any form or by any means, including photocopying, recording, or other electronic or mechanical methods, without the prior written permission of the publisher, except in the case of brief quotations embodied in critical reviews and certain other noncommercial uses permitted by copyright law. For permission requests, write to the author, addressed "Attention: Permissions Coordinator," to the authors website below.

ISBN: 978-1-7359615-2-1

Names, characters, and places are products of the author's imagination.
Front cover image, illustrations, and book design by Stefanie Geyer.
Published in the United States of America.
First printing edition 2021.

Visit the authors website: www.lookbeyondtheclouds.com
To connect on social media, join Michelle's Instagram community @Michelle_Gano
To see more from the illustrator, join Stefanie's Instagram community @Stefanie_Taylor_Art

To my children & students-
I'll never stop believing in you.

"I'm so bad at this. I can't do it," Logan said as he completed his morning work.

"Maybe you can't do it yet, but it'll get better the more you practice," his teacher, Mrs. Honey, said.

"It never gets better for me," Logan mumbled.

Later that day, Logan's classmates were playing soccer during recess. On most days, he sat by himself, but today he decided to play with the other kids.

He ended up kicking the ball into the wrong goal.
One of his teammates yelled, "What did you do, Logan?"

Logan's shoulders lowered as he walked away. Mrs. Honey saw this and went over to him.

Mrs. Honey said, "When I look at you, I see how talented you are. I know what might help you. It's called Teacher Magic. I'll show you how it works."

She waved her hands over his head and said, "A sprinkle of Teacher Magic gives you the power to believe in yourself and keep trying even when you think you can't do something."

She continued, "Words are very powerful. When you tell yourself you can't do something, then your brain won't try and gives up. When you tell yourself you CAN do something, then your brain keeps trying until it finds a solution. Try saying this:
"I BELIEVE IN MYSELF AND I'LL KEEP TRYING."

When they returned to their classroom, it was time for math. Logan felt stuck on a word problem and wanted to give up. Then he remembered Teacher Magic.

He tried one solution, but it didn't work. He tried another and another until finally, he did it.
Maybe Teacher Magic really does help, he thought.

"I BELIEVE IN MYSELF AND I'LL KEEP TRYING."

When the lesson was over, Mrs. Honey asked the class to come to the carpet and close their eyes.

She said, "Think of a time when you felt like you weren't good at something. Raise your hand if that has happened to you."

She paused for a moment and said,
"Keep your hands raised and open your eyes.
What do you notice?"

They looked around, realizing something special.
They were not alone.

Mrs. Honey whispered, "I have something that can help you when you're feeling that way. It's called Teacher Magic."

Logan said quietly, "A sprinkle of Teacher Magic gives you the power to believe in yourself and keep trying even when you think you can't do something." His classmates leaned in as they listened carefully.

Those words are like magic. The more you say it, then the more you'll believe it. The next time any of you think you can't do something, try saying that and see what happens."

The next day when Logan entered the classroom, he noticed his classmate was upset.
He asked, "What happened?"

"I miss my mom and can't get through the day without her," she explained.

In that moment, Logan realized something special. He could share the magic that's in his heart with others, just like Mrs. Honey did for him.

THINK ABOUT IT

- Have you ever felt like you weren't good at something?

- Who has helped you keep trying when you wanted to give up?

NOW IT'S YOUR TURN

- Say, "I believe in myself and I'll keep trying," the next time you think you can't do something.

- Spread this magic to your friends and family by teaching them how powerful their words can be.

YOUR FREE GIFT

If you love coloring as much as I do,
download your own Teacher Magic coloring pages at
www.lookbeyondtheclouds.com/resources.

ABOUT THE AUTHOR

Michelle Gano has a special way of finding the good in each day, which inspires other people to do the same. She enjoys the simple moments in life like watching a beautiful sunrise or spending time with her husband, children, and puppy.

You can find Michelle singing and dancing around the house to Disney songs or making crafts with her family. She believes glitter makes crafts -and the world- a more magical place.

As a teacher, she has touched the lives of many students and families over the years. She taught beyond academics and made sure her students always felt loved and cared for. Now, she continues to spread love and joy to children everywhere through her books.

Learn more about Michelle at www.lookbeyondtheclouds.com.

ABOUT THE ILLUSTRATOR

Stefanie Geyer is a children's book illustrator from Winamac, Indiana. When she's not making beautiful illustrations, you can find her enjoying nature, hiking in the woods, and gardening. She loves photography, traditional drawing, and home renovation projects.

Stefanie is an avid animal lover. She lives with Chris and their five dogs, Halen, Presley, Kimber, Roux, and Draco. Her artwork inspires children to be creative and explore their own love of art.

Learn more about Stefanie on Instagram @Stefanie_Taylor_Art

A SPECIAL NOTE

Dear parents & teachers,

Thank you for reading this book with your children. Society seems to damage their self-esteem at a young age. It's up to us to help them learn the importance of believing in themselves so they can take on life's adventures with confidence.

At times, you might even feel like Logan. Always remember, the magic is in your heart, too. Your little angels look up to you so next time you feel stuck try saying this: "I believe in myself and I'll keep trying."

Thank you for loving your children the way you do and for believing in them until they can believe in themselves!

www.ingramcontent.com/pod-product-compliance
Lightning Source LLC
Chambersburg PA
CBHW042256100526
44589CB00002B/38